Wind of Expression

Rowley Samuels Jr.

Inspiring Voices®

A Service of **Guideposts**

Inspiring Voices books may be ordered through booksellers or by contacting:

Inspiring Voices
1663 Liberty Drive
Bloomington, IN 47403
www.inspiringvoices.com
1-(866) 697-5313

ISBN: 978-1-4624-0449-0 (sc)
ISBN: 978-1-4624-0450-6 (e)

Library of Congress Control Number: 2012922691

Printed in the United States of America

Inspiring Voices rev. date:12/17/2012

Wind of Expression

Hello my name is Rowley Samuels Jr.

TIME

Time has life in a hour glass,
and sand has it's passion.

Love is ours !
and time hold the answer,

to if you'll be mine.
time is funny,

And there was a time when I didn't think I was gonna find
you.
People rushing though life,

Find that the thing they love the most is the one thing they
can't have !
and I'm so glad I can have you.

Your looks- Encanting

The thought of being with you- excites me

Time without you is- Unbearable

I sat here for a time wrote out my thoughts and wondered if time would be ours.

I'm a writer

Expression

This is about a man who is not allowed to show feeling,
am I not allowed to have tears of joy ?

Can't I be sad the rain falls ?
Can I yearn to have you love me just alittle bit more.

Why do people think because I'm Mr.Nice Guy
I can't get mad !

Or because I stand alone I don't need love.
Just because I can't put my words together doesn't mean I
don't wanna talk,

Maybe I'm scared to show my feelings for fear someone
might see !
Why is everyone watching me ?

Can't they see what I've been able to see the whole time,
that I need the chance to express myself even more then they
do.

Because I can't !

I write poetry

A lifetime

It took a lifetime to get you,
it took a lifetime for me to tell you how I feel.

And even longer for me to show you !
How long will it take me to show you ?

By the time I'm finish we'll be in heaven an hour.
So let me tell you I love you as much as I want to,

cause life is so short !
And it's already taken a lifetime.

To make a dream,
so let spend the rest of our life making the dream come true.

I'll never do anything make the dream end,
and please don't you do anything to make it end.

Cause when it takes a lifetime to get something,
that's something you hold on to

Cause it's the best thing you have in your life !
so hold on to it

Cause life is short.
And it already taken us a lifetime.

So let spend the rest of our life in love.

Sometimes I can get creative

I remember paradise

Here I am with that same old feeling,
that feeling where I feel like I'm on the outside of life looking
in.

I can feel the pain in my heart when I see you standing
there,
and I yearn for the way it use to be !

cause I remember paradise
When we would sit and talk for hours.

All I get now is a quick phone call,and fast vistation.
I look at you, and you tell me to stop looking at you !

but I remember paradise
When I would look at you and you would wink and blow me
a kiss.

Yes I remember paradise
When we were falling in love

Where did yesterday go ?
and why did it end so soon ?

I guess it was something that was before it's time.
I would only go back to paradise with you,

Cause it felt so good and it felt so right !
I remember paradise

Can you remember when we fell in love ?
now that was paradise to me.

True love

This is about true love,
something a person doesn't find everyday.

I know,cause my true love was with me for five years.
Well I thought she was my true love !

because she was my first love,
so I did what I thought people did when they are in love.

But little did I know all I was doing was proving myself,
but like the old saying goes,"If you love someone you should
set them free."

"and if they love you they'll come back, and they're your's
forever"
so I set her free, and one day the phone rang.

It was her asking can she come over.
Three years had passed since I saw her !

But I was playin the role of a playa,
but then I saw her. The so call playa was reduced to a man in
love !

and three years of love came pouring out,
and the so called playa found out what true love was all
about.

And sometimes I brag in my peotry

My Wish

If I had one wish,
diamonds and furs.

I don't need all that stuff!
all I need is you in my life.

Yeah one wish my wish,
would be to wake up everyday of my life with you by my
side.

To walk down the road of love holding your hand,
One wish my wish

Would be to fall asleep every night with my head on your
shoulder.
One wish my wish

Is not for diamonds or pearls emeralds nor furs,
my wish is a life with you !

So keep the precious stones and all the things that would
make one rich,
you'll be my jewel.

I'll look at you cause my wish would be a life with you

All the time I write about feelings

You wasn't feeling me

I saw you standing there,
I thought you were the love of my life.

But you wasn't feeling me !
having you was like living a dream,

Having the life I always wanted.
I was lovin you,

but you wasn't feeling me !
What did I do wrong ?

and how do I get it back ?
or did I ever have it ?

I thought you were the love of my life,
a dream come true.

but you wasn't feeling me !
I saw you standing there,

And life started to change.
I thought you were for me,

but you wasn't feeling me !
I cried in wonder of why you didn't feel for me as I felt for
you.

I thought you were the love of my life,
a dream come true.

The life I always wanted,
but you wasn't feeling me !

I also write about dreams

Part of my dream

I was walking down a dark path,
it was full of bad things !

It was dark and scary.
I heard a gun shot !

and I started to run.
All I could do is think of you,

I ran down the path.
and I saw a man as white as light !

I ran toward him,
and he pulled out a knife.

I saw it just before he tried to put it in me !
I slipped and went though him.

I rush down the path,
and I saw a snake.

Then I change directions,
I ran and I stopped !

Still thinking of you.
All at once I saw a street,

made of gold !
I stepped on it,

and I woke up.
And I saw you laying there.

I said to you,
"Have you ever had a dream so good you spent your whole
life trying to get back to it ?"

She said"No."
Thanks for being part of my dream.

This poem is about a man falling in love

A million stars

There's a million stars in the sky tonight,
but there a million stars in the sky every night.

People walking around never taking time to look at the sky,
and it's a pity !

cause it's so beautiful.
Especially at night.

I met a girl tonight,
she showed me the beauty in the sky.

It was the first time I saw it !
people look up without ever seeing.

But there's a million stars in the sky tonight,
but there's a million stars in the sky every night !

Yeah but this is the first time I notice it.

This poem was going though my head one night

Real strength

Sometimes in a man's life, there a time when he feels like he doesn't have a friend.
A time he walks though life with his head high and his heart low !

And when he's alone you can hear him cry,
and though his tears you can see the pain.

The pain of his wants,
the pain of all his desires.

He needs to rest,
but he can't rest.

Not until his needs are met !
He wants to give up at times,

But there's voices in his head telling him not to,
he need the love that is not there.

Cause he feels weak !
and that's when his strength comes in.

And alot times he'll fall,
but he'll always get up and fight the fight that's kept him
down for so long.

I wrote about hurt

Hurt

I know you're hurt,
because of what I did.

I know you're hurt,
because of the things I can't do !

but I love you with all my heart,
and I'll always do my best for you.

The word no hurts,
but it doesn't mean I don't care !

I know the feeling of pain in a heart that doesn't feel love,
I know the love is lock somewhere inside.

I can see the love when I look in your eyes !
but to see the love, and to feel the love are two different
things.

I know you're hurt for what I did,
I know you're hurt for what I can't do.

And I realize,
but you have to realize I'm hurt too.

This poem started to be about one thing,but turned out to be about something else.

Out of the darkness

I remember a day that was full of darkness.
A day I walked along the street, and cried !

I cried cause I could feel the pain,
the pain of being without her.

I didn't see the need to go on,
as I opened the door

I couldn't see the light.
It was so dark !

I was so scared,
I thought I would never see her again.

I walked along crying and longing for the day I could see her again,
but just when the sky was at it's darkest.

I could feel something telling me to turn and look,
so I started the turn !

and I saw a little round light,
that got bigger with every motion of the turn.

So as I complated the turn,
I saw her standing there.

She looked even prettier then I remembered !
I looked at her, and she looked at me.

I called her name,
and she said Hi !

The lights were really bright.
As I came from the darkness into the light,

she was there to greet me.

This poem is from a series of poems

Minute by minute

I'm down,
I use to take life one day at a time !

but since you been gone I take it minute by minute.
Minute by minute is how I live my life,

cause one minute your up and the next your down.
I have to find something to feel good about life again !

You were the only one that made me feel good about
everything,
but now that your gone I see things the way I use to before I
met you !

taking life one day at a time,
but now I take it minute by minute.

This is another poem from that Series of poems

Outer shell

It's time to put on my outer shell,
it's time to get ready for the hurt.

I know it's coming !
cause I think I made a mistake when I did what I did.

So put on my outer shell,
cause it's coming !

And it's gonna hurt bad,
and I'll be embarrassed.

I wish I could go somewhere else,
so I don't feel it !

I hope my outer shell is strong enough to protect me,
cause it's been though so many battles.

trying to protect me !
trying to get to the time when I don't have to use it.

Come on outer shell protect me again !

I wrote this poem for a girlfriend I had at the time

The jewel of my life

My writing is something that's emotional,
if it's not emotional I can't write about it.

I guess that's why I write about you so well !
cause it's something that's emotional to me.

You were someone I thought was very pretty,
and I was so shy !

but that didn't stop me from wanting to be with you.
I use to walk outside at night and wish upon the stars that I
would see you,

and I would think of things to say to you.
But when I saw you all I could do is look at the beauty,

and admire something I thought I could never have !
you were like a priceless stone in a jewelry store window,

That I couldn't afford !
but now you're the jewel of my life.

Sometimes I meet girls online that inspire

Cyber angel

I remember I started to hang in cyber space,
I went to alot of sites.

There were alot of people there who talked about me,and
cussed me out !
and called me names.

I was about to give up on cyber space,
then I went to this site called 2singlepeople !

and I met a cyber angel.
We started sending messages to each other everyday,

She's one in million !
and I'm RJC.

I never thought they had gold in cyber space,
and I never thought I'd find a angel.

You know the internet didn't get good until I met you
Roxanna.
You are my cyber angel. A cyber dream come true !

This is a poem I wrote when I was thinking about a ex-girlfriend

Bag of emotion

Bag of emotion, that's how I feel for you.
When your not around I don't love you !

but when we're together love shines bright.
Do you care for her,someone would ask.

And I would say no !
But when your in town we'll walk down the street hand and
hand.

I'm gonna tell you the truth, I love you with all my heart
and I always will.

I hate you !
but when your here I'll love you better then anyone has ever
loved you.

No I don't love her,
but when you ask me.

Yes I do love you and I always will !
so if you hear my friends say he don't love you.

That's just my way of making it until I get to you

This poem is what my writing this book is about

Feelings

It's easy to tell your love you don't love her anymore,
it's easy to say go away.

But the feelings you had when you started are still there !
and will never fade.

Cause when you love someone alot of things are easy,
but what's hard is not to show the expression on your face
when you see each other.

and hard to lie about what is in your heart.
Yes it's easy to tell your love you don't love her anymore,

It's easy to say go away !
But it's hard not to show the expression of your feelings

This is a poem of what this book is about too

Dreams

Have you ever had a dream ?
did that dream come true ?

Do you know what it feels like to have a dream come true ?
My dream came true the day I met you.

And then the real dream begun,
a walk in the park.

Time spent with you !
The real dream is a life with you.

I've dreamt of a life with you,
house in the suburb three kids the whole 9

Dreams.

This last poem wasn't like the rest, it was written on the spot
as I put it in the book

I did that

I write songs, I write poetry that made my life come alive.
I walked the streets looking for creativity !

I wrote the words to explan my life,
I did that !

When it came to me feeling good about life that's what I did.
I wrote words to express my ups and downs !

everyone has they're way of making it though life,
and this is my claim to fame.

People didn't know what I was up to,
but they were not to know,

and now the secret out !
and this is what I do.

I can paint a picture with words,
I take my experiences and make it creativity !

I take words and creat a way of life

Printed in the United States
by Bookmasters

Printed in the United States
By Bookmasters